Please visit our website, www.garethstevens.com. For a free color catalog of all our high-quality books, call toll free 1-800-542-2595 or fax 1-877-542-2596.

Cataloging-in-Publication Data

Names: Machajewski, Sarah.
Title: Brown recluse spiders / Sarah Machajewski.
Description: New York : Gareth Stevens Publishing, 2018. | Series: Spiders: eight-legged terrors | Includes index.
Identifiers: ISBN 9781538202029 (pbk.) | ISBN 9781538202036 (library bound) | ISBN 9781538202920 (6 pack)
Subjects: LCSH: Brown recluse spider–Juvenile literature.
Classification: LCC QL458.42.L6 M33 2018 | DDC 595.4'4–dc23

First Edition

Published in 2018 by
Gareth Stevens Publishing
111 East 14th Street, Suite 349
New York, NY 10003

Copyright © 2018 Gareth Stevens Publishing

Designer: Laura Bowen
Editor: Ryan Nagelhout

Photo credits: Cover, pp. 1, 13 (spider) Robert Noonan/Getty Images; cover, pp. 1-24 (background) Fantom666/Shutterstock.com; cover, pp. 1-24 (black splatter) Miloje/Shutterstock.com; cover, pp. 1-24 (web) Ramona Kaulitzki/Shutterstock.com; pp. 4-24 (text boxes) Tueris/Shutterstock.com; p. 4 Mithril/Wikimedia Commons; p. 5 S Camazine/K Visscher/Getty Images; p. 7 (daddy longlegs) Paul Looyen/Shutterstock.com; p. 7 (scorpion) CHAIUDON/Shutterstock.com; p. 7 (mite) schankz/Shutterstock.com; p. 7 (tick) Aka/Wikimedia Commons; p. 9 (body) Jernigan,Larry F./Getty Images; pp. 9 (eyes), 19 (top) Kopiersperre/Wikimedia Commons; p. 15 SMC Images/Getty Images; p. 17 SCOTT CAMAZINE/Getty Images; p. 19 (bottom) Chaldor/Wikimedia Commons.

All rights reserved. No part of this book may be reproduced in any form without permission in writing from the publisher, except by a reviewer.

Printed in China

CPSIA compliance information: Batch #CS17GS: For further information contact Gareth Stevens, New York, New York at 1-800-542-2595.

CONTENTS

Watch Out for the Brown Recluse! 4

Awful Arachnids 6

Very Scary Violins 8

Where to Find Them 10

A True Recluse 12

On the Hunt 14

Scary Spiderlings 16

A Bite That Kills Skin 18

Malicious or Misunderstood? 20

Glossary 22

For More Information 23

Index 24

Words in the glossary appear in **bold** type the first time they are used in the text.

WATCH OUT FOR THE BROWN RECLUSE!

Watch out if you ever find yourself going through one of these places: under a pile of boards, deep in your closet, or in a corner of your attic. You may find yourself face-to-face with a brown recluse spider.

Brown recluse spiders have a bad **reputation**. These eight-legged terrors are small, but scary. And their bite can be very serious. But they're also shy, and they're probably more afraid of us than we are of them! Let's learn more about this amazing animal.

Watch out for the brown recluse spider!

AWFUL ARACHNIDS

There are more than 43,000 species, or kinds, of spiders living in the world. The brown recluse is just one species, but it's widely known because of its poisonous bite.

Spiders are part of an animal group called arachnids. Daddy longlegs, scorpions, ticks, and mites belong to this group, too. It's safe to say that arachnids aren't the most popular animals around—especially spiders. Though most are harmless, coming across even the tiniest spider is enough to make some people scream!

TERRIFYING TRUTHS

The largest daddy longlegs can have legs as long as 5.9 inches (15 cm)!

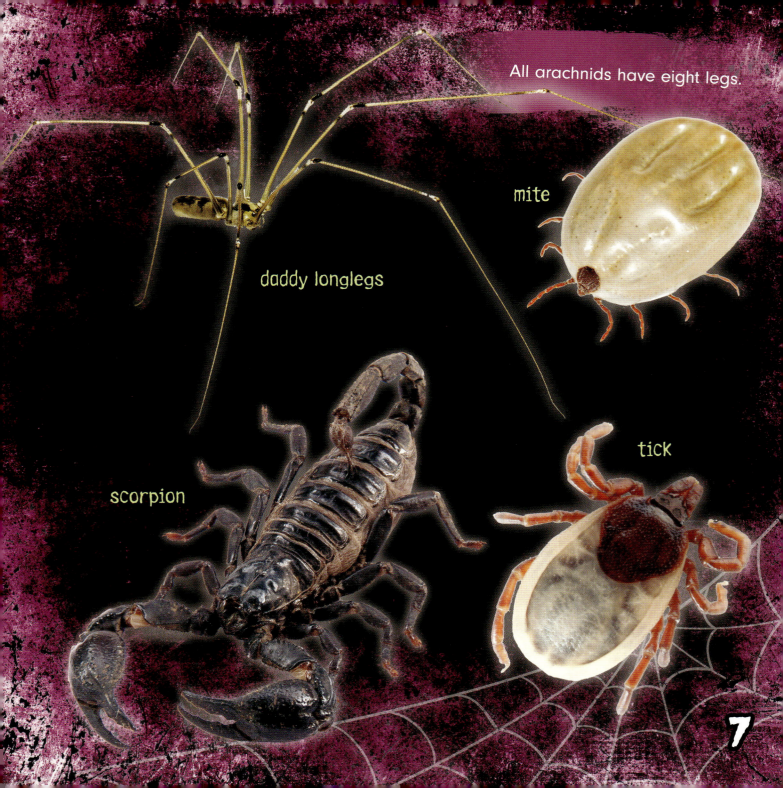

VERY SCARY VIOLINS

Brown recluse spiders are brown and bad, but not very big. These furry creatures are about 3/8 inch (1 cm) long and 3/16 inch (0.5 cm) wide.

Unlike other spiders, the brown recluse has six eyes. Its eyes are arranged in three pairs across its head. Also, on its head are **distinctive** markings that look like a violin. The violin shape can be hard to see, but the eyes don't lie. When you see six, it's definitely a brown recluse.

TERRIFYING TRUTHS

Brown recluse spiders are one of the few venomous spiders in the United States.

PARTS OF A BROWN RECLUSE SPIDER

eyes

leg

brown fur

violin-shaped markings

Brown recluse spiders have a few special features that help scientists and doctors recognize them.

WHERE TO FIND THEM

Brown spiders live all over the place. When you see one, you might be scared it's a brown recluse. But while this species is the most common of the brown spiders, it doesn't live all over. Its habitat, or where it lives, is mostly in the southern and central United States.

It's unusual to see it outside this area, but it's sometimes found in southern Canada. These spiders can also be carried to other places if they're hiding in something, such as a moving box.

TERRIFYING TRUTHS

Brown recluse spiders are native to the United States. Some other brown spider species have been brought to North America from other countries.

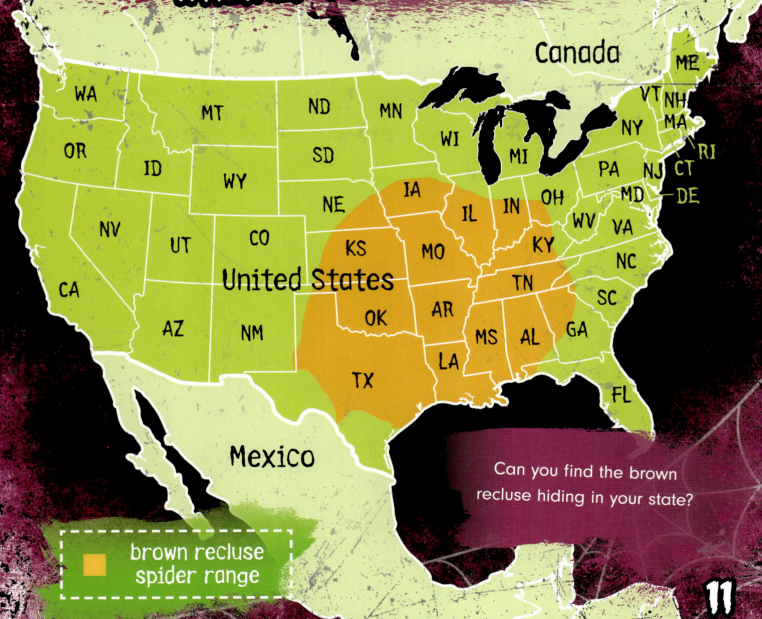

A TRUE RECLUSE

You can learn a lot about brown recluse spiders by thinking about their name. A recluse is someone who avoids people, preferring to live alone. This is exactly how the spider behaves!

Brown recluse spiders are solitary creatures, which means they live alone. They spend much of their time hiding in dark places. In the wild, these spiders live under logs and rocks. You might find them in boxes, piles of clothing, furniture, old tires, and maybe even inside your shoe!

TERRIFYING TRUTHS

Brown recluse spiders are nocturnal, which means they're active at night and hide during the day. You may not even know they're there!

Brown recluse spiders love places that sit undisturbed for a long time. They've even been found in people's bedsheets. Yikes!

ON THE HUNT

Many spiders are known for the silky webs they **weave** to catch **prey**. Spider webs are commonly very strong so they can be good traps for bugs. Most web-weaving spiders wait in their web until their prey comes along, but the brown recluse catches prey a bit differently.

The brown recluse spider doesn't use its web to catch food. Instead, it's a hunter, searching for and preying on bugs both dead and alive. When it bites, the spider's **fangs** release toxic venom that kills.

TERRIFYING TRUTHS

The brown recluse spider is a great survivor. It can last months without food and water.

Brown recluse spider webs are loose and not orderly. They're built low to the ground or in hidden corners. The webs are used for nesting, not for hunting.

SCARY SPIDERLINGS

Brown recluse spiders like to be alone, but many are often found living together or near each other. **Infestations** happen quickly because female spiders lay 40 to 50 eggs at a time!

Female spiders weave an egg sac into their web. Spider eggs hatch into tiny spiders called spiderlings. They slowly get bigger over time through a process called **molting**. This happens between five and eight times until they become adults.

TERRIFYING TRUTHS

Female spiders can produce up to five egg sacs in their life. That can lead to hundreds of brown recluse spiders and one bad infestation!

The skin left behind by brown recluse spiders molting can be a sign of a spider infestation!

A BITE THAT KILLS SKIN

Many people fear the brown recluse spider because of its bite. The spider bites when it feels threatened, such as when you put on a shoe it's chosen to nest in or if you roll over one that's hiding in your bed.

People don't commonly feel the bite when it happens, though, and **symptoms** take hours to set in. The bite soon becomes red, swollen, and sore. A **blister** may appear, and some people start to feel sick.

TERRIFYING TRUTHS

A brown recluse spider bite can make people really sick. It can cause pain and chills and make you throw up.

brown recluse fangs

In the worst cases, a brown recluse spider bite may cause a person's skin to become necrotic. That means the skin cells die, and the skin turns black and purple!

MALICIOUS OR MISUNDERSTOOD?

Brown recluse spiders have a bad reputation, and it's easy to see why. Their bite is poisonous. They can cause a lot of pain and sickness. And they hide, creeping around and hatching spiderlings where we can't see them.

These facts make the brown recluse seem like a true terror, but, believe it or not, they're not entirely bad. Spiders hunt bugs, which controls the pest population. And brown recluse spiders are more afraid of us than we are of them. They just want to be left alone! But if you see one, watch out. These eight-legged terrors are still willing to bite.

HANDLING THE BITE OF A BROWN RECLUSE SPIDER

SIGNS:
- red, itchy skin
- blister or sore with irregular edges
- skin turning black or purple

SYMPTOMS:
- fever
- chills
- throwing up
- headache
- itching

TIME:
- Symptoms appear 3 to 8 hours after the bite occurs.
- The bite usually takes about 3 weeks to heal.
- Some lasting **scarring** may occur.

NEXT STEPS:
- If you think you've been bitten, tell an adult immediately.
- Put ice on the bite.
- Get to the doctor right away!

GLOSSARY

blister: a painful swelling on the skin

distinctive: a feature of something that sets it apart from others

fang: a hard, sharp-pointed body part a spider uses to put venom in its prey

fever: a raised body temperature due to sickness

headache: pain in the head

infestation: an unusually large number of bugs or animals in one place, typically causing damage or sickness

itch: the need to scratch something

molting: to shed skin, fur, or feathers in order to make way for new growth

prey: an animal that's hunted by other animals for food

reputation: the views that are held about something or someone

scar: a mark left on the skin after injury

symptom: a sign that shows someone is sick

weave: to make by twining threads together

FOR MORE INFORMATION

BOOKS

Amstutz, Lisa J. *Spiders*. North Mankato, MN: Capstone Press, 2018.

de la Bédoyère, Camilla. *Mini Monsters*. Irvine, CA: QEB Publishing, 2012.

Evans, Janet. *Spiders: 101 Fun Facts and Amazing Pictures*. Newark, DE: Speedy Kids, 2013.

WEBSITES

Brown Recluse Spider
spidersworlds.com/brown-recluse-spider/
Find out more about the brown recluse spider here.

Brown Recluse Spider
kidzone.ws/lw/spiders/facts-brownrecluse.htm
Take a closer look at the brown recluse spider on this site.

Hey! A Brown Recluse Spider Bit Me!
kidshealth.org/en/kids/brown-recluse.html
Kid's Health examines brown recluse spiders and the steps to take if you find one.

Publisher's note to educators and parents: Our editors have carefully reviewed these websites to ensure that they are suitable for students. Many websites change frequently, however, and we cannot guarantee that a site's future contents will continue to meet our high standards of quality and educational value. Be advised that students should be closely supervised whenever they access the Internet.

INDEX

arachnids 6, 7

bite 4, 18, 19, 20, 21

blister 18, 21

eggs 16

egg sacs 16

eyes 8

fangs 14

female spiders 16

habitat 10

hunter 14

infestations 16, 17

molting 16, 17

nesting 15, 18

prey 14

solitary creatures 12

species 6, 10

spiderlings 16, 20

symptoms 18, 21

venom 8, 14

violin 8

webs 14, 15